Fixing our Eyes on Jesus Series

The Secret

of

Gaining Wisdom

...

Ask God for It!

By Teddy James O'Farrell

Copyright ©2020 by Teddy James O'Farrell

FIRST EDITION

www.teddyofarrell.com

ISBN:978-1-7362956-0-1

A PDF Download is available from teddyofarrell.com.
Copyright @2020 by Teddy James O'Farrell

Rev. Teddy James O'Farrell
The Alliance Church of Zephyrhills
6251 Fort King Road
Zephyrhills   FL 33542
www.teddyofarrell.com
www.zaccma.org
813-782-8865

All scripture quotations, unless otherwise showed, come from the Holy Bible: NIV Holy Bible, New International Version®, NIV®.

To all the men and women who have spent a lifetime on their knees, seeking God's wisdom. Thank you for your example of the Christian Faith.

Table of Contents

Prologue

We live in a world today that is crying for wisdom. Knowledge has increased exponentially since the turn of the century. Even now, the thirst for information and knowledge shows all who turn to the internet daily. But "knowledge" is not wisdom. Neither is information. Although both are building blocks for discernment and helping one make the right decisions. "Wisdom," is different. It is the opinion of this author that, "Wisdom" is far superior to the other two. However, wisdom incorporates knowledge and information and intelligence. Wisdom is putting into practice what one has learned and what one can apply to his or her own life. In the Pastoral Epistles, the Book of James, who wrote a letter to believers, stated, "If any of you lacks wisdom let them ask of God who gives to all generously, without finding fault" (James 1:5). Here is the secret of gaining wisdom; it is asking God for it through prayer.

Our church started on a journey to seek God's wisdom. We began by studying the Old Testament Book of Proverbs. Similar to the New Testament Book of James, Proverbs has much to offer in gaining an understanding of wisdom. It reveals how to ask God for it. The following pages are prayers based on each chapter of Proverbs. My desire is for each prayer to deepen one's relationship with God. My prayer is for those who read them, that they will be more than just words. These prayers will become your prayers as you seek to gain an understanding of wisdom. God will answer your prayers. Remember, He gives generously to those who ask! May you discover a rich inheritance of God's wisdom in the following pages.

Asking God together,
Teddy James O'Farrell
December 2020

Proverbs 1.

For Gaining Wisdom and Instruction

Dear Heavenly Father,

As I look into your Word, I pray that you will give me wisdom and instruction. May Your Holy Spirit provide me with insight so I will know how to act and behave! Your Wisdom, in me, will help me do what is right, just and fair.

I pray that I may have prudence, knowledge and discretion, let these be the building blocks for applying your truth and wisdom in my life. You grant discernment to those who listen to you and give guidance to those who seek You. Lord, I am asking you now. I am waiting to hear your voice speak.

Thank you for understanding the message of your words found in scripture.

May your Spirit fall fresh on me and give a deeper reverence and "awe" of who You are! The beginning of wisdom is discovering more of You.

Thank you for my parent's example of teaching me your ways. They blessed my family and me like a garland that graces my head. I praise you for their pattern of living a godly life.

Keep me from sinful men and let their speech not sway me. No matter how great they promise to gain wealth, keep my eyes on You. Those who seek selfishness or ill-gotten gain will lose their life, but those who seek You will live. Help me seek first the Kingdom of God and Your righteousness.

Let me hear wisdom's voice and calling, and may I listen, learn, and obey. There are those who mock and hate your truth, grant

me the ability not to join in with them. Let
me not be the one whom you laugh at,
Lord, when disaster strikes or when calamity
overtakes. But I ask that You Lord will be
near me. When I call, You will answer, I
will find you as I look for You. You will
hear my prayers and answer because I fear
Your Holy Name.

"MAY YOUR SPIRIT FALL FRESH ON ME... THE BEGINNING OF WISDOM IS DISCOVERING MORE OF YOU!"

Keep me as the apple of your eye, let me
trust and obey your advice. Let my life
bring you praise and honor in all I do and
say. Help me not become complacent or be
lead astray.

Let me listen to You; be my wisdom. Then
I know I will live in safety and be at ease
without being afraid.   Thank you for your
presence and your protection.

In Jesus' Name

INSIGHTS IN CHAPTER 1

Verses 1 through 7 gives the theme of the
entire book which is gaining "wisdom."

A Key Verse for this chapter is verse 7,

*"The fear of the Lord is the beginning of
knowledge, but fools despise wisdom and
instruction." (NIV)*

HELPFUL HINT: Try memorizing
Proverbs 1:7 this week!

Proverbs 2.
Fathers' Advice

Dear Heavenly Father,

Help me accept what you say and apply your instructions for my life. Let me hear your wisdom. Give me an understanding heart. I want to have your insight and understanding in my life every day. Let me search for them like a hidden treasure, knowing that when I have found them, and I will gain a more excellent knowledge of you and will reverence your Great Name. You are the God of wisdom. Your word gives insight and understanding. You are my source of victory, my protector, my defender, my helper. Let me walk upright, blameless, and just before you. I long to be faithful to you.

When I am faithful, you will grant understanding. I will know what is right, just, and fair. You are the source of true discernment. Your wisdom will enter my heart, and your knowledge will please my soul. Your understanding is too fantastic for me. I enjoy being in your Holy presence. Grant me discretion that will protect and guard my heart against misunderstanding.

Let me not get distracted or caught up with the ways of the wicked. Help me walk in faith, following your steps along your lighted path. Keep me from being influenced by those who delight in doing wrong. Keep me from being carried off by those who take joy in being perverse and evil.

Let me be one of your children who walks on the straight and narrow path, avoiding the crooked road that leads to destruction. Keep me faithful and right in my relationships with others. Give me an undivided heart that I may fear your Name.

Let your wisdom save me from wandering away from you. Help me keep my commitments and promises to You.

"YOUR WISDOM WILL ENTER MY HEART, AND YOUR KNOWLEDGE WILL PLEASE MY SOUL."

Give me an understanding heart that I may grieve for those who are on the path that leads to death - I pray that You Almighty God will reduce them from their sin-filled ways.

Keep my attention and focus on You so I may walk on the path of the righteous, that I will live and be blameless — for You give life, You cleanse and heal and restore and consider me blameless in your sight. Thank you for interceding on my behalf, for continuing to work—your good work in me.

In Jesus' Name

<u>INSIGHTS IN CHAPTER 2</u>

This chapter begins as if a Father is giving his son timely advice on how to live successfully. Notice verse 1, "If you…" and verse 5, "then you…" Listening and obeying are building blocks in gaining wisdom.

A Key Verse for this chapter is verse 6

"For the Lord gives wisdom; from his mouth come knowledge and understanding." (NIV)

HELPFUL HINT: Try memorizing Proverbs 2:6 this week!

Proverbs 3.
Trusting the Lord

Dear Heavenly Father,

There is a longing in my heart to listen to your voice, giving me instruction. Teach me your ways, that I may follow them, for your commands give life and bring peace and prosperity. Help me be faithful and loving; may these attributes become core truths in my heart and soul. May they complement my reputation! In doing so, may I win favor and a well-respected name in your sight!

May I trust in you with all my heart and truly not rely on my insight or understanding. Forgive me of the times when I try even to figure you out. Help me submit to you, my Lord, knowing that you will lead me in paths of righteousness for your namesake. Your ways are straight and true. I bow in reverence and worship you.

Help me stay away from evil and think soberly about who I am, not boastful or proud. You will take care of my reputation and what others think of me, let me be content in being your child. Your watch-care over me will bring health to my body and soul.

May I honor you, Lord, with all that you provide for me, as an offering and testimony of your love, greatness, faithfulness, and blessing! As I do, you will keep on filling and providing for all my needs to the point of over-flowing abundance. How wonderful you are!

Grant me the acceptance to receive your discipline and correction, knowing that you love me when you correct me. Just as a father delights in his son, you delight in me.

Give me an understanding heart and bless me with your wisdom. It is worth more than silver and gold. It is more precious than rubies. Help me value "wisdom" above anything else, for You give long life, wealth, and honor to those who put You first.   May my life exhibit peace as I put your truth into practice. Your wisdom is far greater than a man's wisdom. You, Oh Lord, laid the earth's foundations and set the heaven's in place. You made the land and the sea, the clouds and the stars. You are my Creator, blessed be Your Name. Help me keep focused on seeking your wisdom. Give me the ability to guard sound judgment and discretion.   May they complement my life.

"teach me your ways…"

Thank you for your protection that when I lie down, I will not be afraid, and my rest will be sweet. I will not fear of sudden disaster or of the ruin that overtakes the wicked, because You are with me. Thank you for being at my side.

Give me a generous heart and show kindness to my neighbors when they are in need. Help me show them your love and truth. Help me hold my tongue and not speak evil or accuse anyone falsely. Keep evil and violence far from the paths I walk on. Let me be upright in your sight. May your blessing fall on my home and family. I will inherit honor and you will count me as one of your wise children when I focus on You.

In Jesus' Name

__INSIGHTS IN CHAPTER 3__

There are great truths throughout this chapter. Pay close attention to verses 3 - 8. Notice keywords like "love, faithfulness, trust, lean-not, health." Love and faithfulness and trust are three more building blocks for gaining wisdom.

A Key Verse for this chapter is verse 5
"Trust in the Lord with all your heart and lean not on your own understanding;" (NIV)

HELPFUL HINT: Try memorizing Proverbs 3:5 this week!

Proverbs 4.
Following the Right Path

Dear Heavenly Father,

Thank you for the wisdom of my parents, help me remember the instructions that reflect your truth, love, and knowledge. Help me pursue Your wisdom and understanding with all my heart, knowing that as I do, you will grant blessing and direction for my life.

May your Word light my path and give guidance as I follow you. May my steps be sure and strong when I walk on your path. When I run, may I run to you, fixing my eyes on you, not stumbling along the way. Keep me focused on You, my Lord, and your teachings.

Do not let me get distracted by the things of this world. Keep me from the path of the wicked. Help me avoid it. Your path is the way of the righteous, help me follow your direction. You are the light of the world. Your word is a light unto my path. Let me walk under your view.

Help me be mindful of your Word. Let your word permeate my thoughts throughout this day. Keep what you say in my sight and write them on my heart. Guard my heart, make me devoted to You. Let my words bring forth praise.

May my conversations become edifying, encouraging, uplifting, and a blessing to others. Let my eyes be on Jesus Christ as I walk and run this race. Help me finish the race and win the prize for the glory of Jesus Christ.

 In Jesus' Name,

"May your Word light my path and give guidance as I follow you!"

INSIGHTS IN CHAPTER 4

Two themes emerge as you read this Proverb. First, get wisdom at any cost (see v.5-6). Second, follow "wisdom" along straight paths. (v.11). The cost of "wisdom" is worth it. It takes discipline and commitment, but the benefits far outweigh the cost. Practicing the "wisdom" of God and the mind of Christ in daily living is priceless!

A Key Verse for this chapter is verse 11 *"I instruct you in the way of wisdom and lead you along straight paths." (NIV)*

HELPFUL HINT: Try memorizing Proverbs 4:11 this week!

Proverbs 5.
Saying and Doing the Right Things!

Dear Heavenly Father,

Let my ears hear your words of wisdom, and may I listen to your voice speak insights to me as I go throughout my day. Grant me discretion and discernment in dealing with others that my conversation would honor you. May my speech and actions reflect your truth and knowledge.

Some seek to live their lives filled with selfish pleasures, — greed, lust, coveting what others have, sexual immorality, sensual indulgence, selfish ambition, drunkenness, impurity, and other sins. Keep me from them. Let those who live their lives this way not draw me into their lifestyle, but let your

Light pierce their hearts and bring them to the place of true repentance. I know those who follow the path of practicing these sins — their lives will end in ruin. Help me live for you and practice Holy Spirit-led righteousness.

Help me by your Spirit to say no to ungodliness and wickedness and say yes to You and your righteousness. Let me be faithful to You. Let me be faithful in all my relationships, devoted, loving, and genuine. Let me enjoy my marriage, my spouse, my children, my grandchildren as You designed. Thank you for them. May they see my love for You, my love for them. Keep me true.

Let Your Joy permeate my home, and Your love flow freely from the spring of Living Water. I am thankful that You, my God, know and see all. You know all my ways — they are in your sight. Nothing escapes You. Grant me the discipline, to be faithful and true, to be loving and kind, to be forgiving and patient. Grant me Your love that rejoices in the truth and is not self-serving. Thank you for your grace and strength.

May even the intimacy of my marriage and family be pleasing to You, giving You glory and honor and praise. May it be a testimony, an example of Your love for Your people.

In Jesus' Name,

"May my speech and actions reflect your truth and Knowledge!"

INSIGHTS IN CHAPTER 5

The author of Proverbs gives his son several warnings in this chapter. He wants to make sure his son is listening (see v. 2, v. 7) First, he wants his son to stay away from sexual immorality (v.3, v.8). Next, he wants his son to listen to his teachers (v. 12,13)! He tells him to be faithful in his marriage (v.15,18-20)! He then reminds his son that God sees and knows everything (v.21).

A Key Verse for this chapter is verse 21

"For your ways are in full view of the Lord, and he examines all your paths." (NIV)

HELPFUL HINT: Try memorizing Proverbs 5:21 this week!

Proverbs 6.
Understanding What God Hates!

Dear Heavenly Father,

I praise you because you are the great provider, the one who meets my needs. With what you have entrusted me, help me be a better steward. Let me be honest in all my business dealings. Let me not become enslaved to others, and if I have wronged anyone, give me the humility and grace to seek their forgiveness and favor. Let the only debt that I owe be that of loving others as you have loved me.

Help me show diligence and discipline, like the ant, learning from its example to store food and gather food at the proper times and season. Let not laziness and lack of sleep keep me from serving you and being productive. When you bless me, help me bless others! I devote my heart to you. Let my speech bring forth truth and honesty — let there be no devious or deceitful ways in my heart or mind. Make my motives pure by your Spirit. Wash me, cleanse me, fill me.

Help me love what you love, oh Lord, and hate what you hate. Keep me from the things that grieve you — haughty eyes, a lying tongue, murder, wicked scheming, eagerness to do evil, lying about others, and stirring up dissension. Instead, may the Spirit flow through me your Holy passionate fruit — love, joy, peace, patience, kindness, goodness, faithfulness, gentleness, and self-control.

Let me honor those things that my mom and dad have taught me. That agreed with your word and your truth. Help me remember them like a necklace around my neck. May you enable me to be faithful and loyal in all my relationships with others. Let not the love of this world, lust, greed, and pride influence me. I know your Word teaches that those who commit adultery lacks judgment and brings destruction. Let me exhibit your wisdom, discretion, and fidelity to show your faithfulness and love in all my relationships.

Thank you for watching over me. When tempted, you provide a way of escape that rescues me. Thank you, that when I slip and fall, you pick me up; you forgive as I confess my sins to before you. Continue to create in me a clean heart, a right spirit, that my life — every area of my life — may bring you glory.

In Jesus' Name

"Help me become diligent and disciplined like the ant!"

<u>INSIGHTS IN CHAPTER 6</u>

Do you want to discover what God likes? Check out verses 16-19. Here Solomon lists seven things that God hates.
Understanding what God loves will move you closer to gaining wisdom for your life.

A Key Verse for this chapter is verse 6

"Go to the ant, you sluggard; consider its ways and be wise!" (NIV)

HELPFUL HINT: Try memorizing Proverbs 6:6 this week!

Proverbs 7.
Not Giving into Temptation

Dear Heavenly Father,

Thank you for your Holy Word. May I store your words up, like one who stores up food for the winter. May I memorize them, may I meditate on them and may they become a part of me as I seek you. May your teachings be the apple of my eye, for in them is life and protection. May your Holy Spirit write them on my heart. May wisdom be a product of my spending time with You and studying your Word.

Your Word gives a wealth of insight and keeps me from falling away from you. May I remember your Word when facing temptation. Keep me from all sins, especially sexual immorality. Your wisdom can provide the only way of escape when faced with wandering away from the faith. Keep me close to You. May my actions continually reflect your knowledge and please you in every way. May I be faithful in my marriage, steadfast in my work, committed to fulfilling the duties of a husband, a father, and a provider. Above all, let me be faithful to you.

Help those who are struggling with sin and temptation. Set them free from whatever entangles them and binds them. Do not let their hearts turn away from your Holy Spirit. Move Oh God among us, convicting and cleansing the world from all iniquity.

Thank you for your presence, your power— giving me the ability to say, No to unrighteousness and Yes to righteousness. Be my strength, keep my eyes fixed on You.

In Jesus' Name,

"May your teachings be the apple of my eyes, for in them is life and protection!"

INSIGHTS IN CHAPTER 7

Why does Solomon repeat his warnings regarding committing adultery and sexual immorality again and again? (see chapters 5, 6, 7) Whenever scripture states a theme over and over, or phrase or specific words — we need to pay careful attention to what we read. Keeping oneself pure by overcoming temptation with scripture is the key to living a victorious Christian life. Here the writer says, "Don't get caught up in the smooth talk of the adulterer…" It's so important to fix our eyes on Jesus (Hebrews 12:1-3). A proper focus helps one gain wisdom in living for Christ.

A Key Verse for this chapter is verse 2

"Keep my commands, and you will live; guard my teachings as the apple of your eye." (NIV)

HELPFUL HINT: Try memorizing Proverbs 7:2 this week!

Proverbs 8.
More Precious than Rubies!

Dear Heavenly Father,

I hear the voice of wisdom crying out, calling, and wanting me to listen. Help me hear and receive what You, the author of Wisdom, is saying. Help me understand wisdom's just words. Let me desire them more than silver or gold or rubies, for nothing compares with gaining Godly wisdom.

Lord, continue your excellent work in my life, molding me and making me more like you. Plant in me the seeds of prudence, knowledge, and discretion. Give me a greater fear of You - to love what you love and hate what you hate. Remove evil, pride, arrogance, and perverse speech. May my conduct be pleasing to you. Grant me Lord your understanding and strengthen me with your power that You may receive all the glory and honor and praise, as you work in and through my life.

Father, by your might, You have set up kings, rulers, and leaders. You have appointed them by Your hand and established them by Your wisdom. May they govern by Your knowledge and create laws that are just. Help our leaders to love you. Through your love, let nations turn to you. Help your church to love you more. Help me love you more and seek you more. Pour out your fruit of wisdom upon me, that I may walk in the way of righteousness, along the paths of justice. Bring blessings to all who call upon You. Provide for your people abundance, make their treasuries full. May all people exalt your name, worship, honor, adore, and praise you forever. Thank you for your provision.

Thank you, God, that from the very beginning of creation, Your wisdom was there — thank you, You have revealed your knowledge throughout all time. Thank you, that Your "wisdom" brings delight day after day, rejoicing in Your presence, celebrating in Your world, and delighting in humanity. Thank you, that Jesus Christ is our wisdom, which comes from you. He is our righteousness, holiness, and redemption. Continue to give me a tender ear, always to help me seek you more each day that your favor may rest on me. Thank you for the gift of everlasting life found in Jesus Christ, my Savior, and Lord.

In Jesus' Name

"Nothing compares with gaining Godly wisdom!"

INSIGHTS IN Chapter 8

Wisdom is crying out in this chapter. Notice that it is a call to all humanity (v.4). It is for all people to set their hearts to pursue and attain it (v.5). Verses 10-11 gives the listener, the reader, a choice: Choose wisdom or not? The one who does, they'll discover "wisdom" is more valuable than silver or gold, more precious than rubies. A life built on this foundation will be stable.

A Key Verse for this chapter is verse 35

"For those who find me find life and receive favor from the Lord." (NIV)

HELPFUL HINT: Try memorizing Proverbs 8:35 this week

Proverbs 9.
Benefits of Gaining Wisdom

Dear Heavenly Father,

As I come before you, I recognize that You are the one who is all-knowing and all-wise. You have blessed your people through your Word. The pages of your Word overflow with "wisdom." When one relies on your "wisdom," they are like the man who has built his house upon the rock. It will stand firm in and through the storms.

Help me depend upon Your wisdom and Your truth. May Jesus, who is the cornerstone, be the foundation of my home. When I hear your "wisdom" call out to me, may I listen! Help me know the difference between the world's wisdom and Your Godly wisdom.

When I hear others speak, Lord, help me understand genuinely. If I must use words to rebuke others, may it be on those who are wise, those who are teachable, for they will become more knowledgeable! Let me speak words motivated by Your love and truth. Help me stay clear of those who "mock" and are bent on living a sinful lifestyle. When others come to me, Lord, to rebuke me, help me be slow to speak and again quick to listen.

Remove those things in my life that grieve You. Teach me to be a righteous man, eager to learn from Your Spirit. Grant me a more deep-seated fear, respect, and reverence of who You are, give me the understanding of Your ways, Oh Lord. As I seek You and follow You, You will bless, for Your wisdom gives added days of life. Thank You for Your "wisdom."

Just as wisdom cries out, so does Folly, help me have a discerning heart and follow Your voice. Give me the discipline to stay away from worthless pursuits. Grant me honesty, purity, humility, and integrity in all my ways. For in Christ, I have everlasting life. Thank you for your gift of salvation and strength to serve You.

In Jesus' Name

"I recognize that You are the one who is all Knowing and all wise!"

INSIGHTS IN CHAPTER 9

There are many benefits to gaining wisdom. The writer here reveals some of them. In verses 7-9, "Wisdom" will help you know when to speak and when not to. If you have "wisdom," you will have a teachable spirit. Arrogance and pride will not be present (see v. 9) In verses 10-12, "Wisdom" will give you understanding, and reverence for God. You will gain many days and years to your life.

A Key Verse for this chapter is verse 10

"The fear of the Lord is the beginning of wisdom, and knowledge of the Holy One is understanding." (NIV)

HELPFUL HINT: Try memorizing Proverbs 9:10 this week!

Proverbs 10.
Standing Firm
Through the Storm

Dear Heavenly Father,

As a wise son brings joy to his father and mother and not grief, may I bring joy to you! Thank you for my parents and their example.

Help me do what is right in your sight, to store up treasures in heaven, not from ill-gotten gain. Thank you for your faithfulness, never letting the righteous go hungry. You have graciously provided for all my needs. Bless your Holy Name.

Help my hands to be diligent, making the most of every opportunity — help me be productive in and out of season. May my life reflect the Lord Jesus Christ, may His

Spirit live in me, that His blessings fall on me — that I may give back to Him all the praise and adoration due His great name.

Thank you, that you call us to remember your righteous acts, and you bless those who do. Help me have a teachable spirit, a wise heart that I may accept your commands. Knowing that as I draw near to you, you Lord will draw near to me and mold my life to be one of integrity.

Keep me from the foolish talk and malicious actions of others. Let my speech be a fountain of life, not seasoned with violence, but gives the fragrance of Christ. Let your love flow through me and cover-up all wrong. Grant me discernment and wise speech that speaks of knowledge and good stewardship. Apply discipline to my life, showing the way to live, pointing others to Jesus Christ and His truth.

Pour in me a teachable spirit. Let my relationship with Christ show that I am grounded, let my words be few. May those around me find encouragement, strength and nourishment in their hearts, drawing closer to the Lord. May the blessing of the Lord continue to fall on me, and all those who are His.

Thank you for hearing what the righteous desire and answering prayer. Thank you for being with the righteous in the storms of life and allowing them the strength to stand. Thank you, you give "life" to those who fear your name. Thank you, that you fill the righteous with your joy. You are my refuge, my firm foundation, my wisdom. May I continue to speak what is fitting and bring honor to your name always.

In Jesus' Name

"Thank you for being with the righteous in the storms of life!"

INSIGHTS IN CHAPTER 10

Here, Solomon records his "proverbs." These are wise statements, usually stated in contrasts or comparisons. As you read this chapter, what verses "jump out" at you? Notice the faithfulness of God in verses 3, 6, 9, 22, 25, 27, 29, 30. He gives strength to those who are facing "trials of many kinds" (see James 1). He is with the righteous, and just as Jesus calmed the storm with the disciples (see Mark 4:35-41). You can trust God to calm the storms that you may face.

A Key Verse for this chapter is verse 25

"When the storm has swept by, the wicked are gone, but the righteous stand firm forever." (NIV)

HELPFUL HINT: Try memorizing Proverbs 10:25 this week!

Proverbs 11.
When the Righteous Prosper

Dear Heavenly Father,

I know you delight in honesty, and with your humility comes wisdom. Place in me your knowledge and integrity that they may guide my life. May others consider me "upright."

Knowing You and your righteousness frees me from the bondage of sin and delivers me from death. You are life; the wealth of this world is worthless. Keep me from pursuing useless things, may my feet walk on paths of righteousness for Your Name's sake.

I produce unfaithfulness when evil desires take captive my heart. Let this never happen. Let my hope be in You and You alone. You bless the righteous, and all the city rejoices — let your blessing fall on me. Give me an understanding heart that withholds my tongue, that keeps a secret, and when appropriate, may I speak words that give guidance and secures victory. Help me look out for the benefits of others by showing kindness and honesty.

May I pursue your righteousness that attains life, and may my heart be blameless. Forgive me for those times when my heart strays from your path. Set me free from all the desires that take me away from you. Produce what is right in me in your sight. Help me be generous, knowing that you will bless, provide, and allow me to prosper.

May I trust in you and you alone, my Lord, not in wealth or money or talent or people — but You! When I do, I know I will thrive like a green leaf! Again, place in my heart and mind your wisdom that I may honor my family, and they may experience your peace.

Give me eyes to see what you love, knowing You love humanity, may I win souls for your glory, that the fruit of my life will produce righteousness. A righteous life, not wood, hay or stubble, but gold - that honors and gives glory to You. Be exalted inwardly and outwardly, I pray.

In Jesus' Name,

"Knowing You and Your righteousness frees me from the bondage of sin!"

INSIGHTS IN CHAPTER 11

The contrast between the righteous and the wicked continues in this chapter of Proverbs. Trouble falls on the wicked, while the behavior spares the righteous (v.8). The righteous flourish (v.10), and the city rejoices. The wicked get destroyed, and people shout in gladness! This contrast is clear in the entire chapter. This outcome tells us it is worth following the Lord and obeying His commands. Notice verse 19, the righteous attain life while those who pursue evil will find death. Jesus Christ gives life abundantly (John 10:10) to all who believe in Him (John 3:16, 6:47). May His Holy Spirit continue to refresh you as you seek and serve Him.

A Key Verse for this chapter is verse 25

"A generous person will prosper; whoever refreshes others will be refreshed." (NIV)

HELPFUL HINT: Try memorizing Proverbs 11:25 this week!

Proverbs 12.
The Favor of the Lord

Dear Heavenly Father,

You are so loving that those you love — you will discipline. Instill in me during those corrective times your knowledge and help me listen and change my behavior so you will receive all the glory and praise. Pour out your favor and blessing upon me, may I please you. Establish my steps in paths of righteousness for your Name's sake.

Thank you for your grace, blessing me with my spouse, who you fill with your spirit and is one of noble character. Her testimony is a compliment to me and exhibits her love for you.

Grant that my plans will be righteous and honoring. Help my speech, and my words will be upright. Use them to rescue the wicked and tell of your salvation. Thank you, that you establish the house of the righteous on a firm foundation. I praise you that Jesus is my cornerstone. Continue to build my life to be a temple of praise. Fill me with your Spirit, that out of my character will flow wisdom, honesty, humility, compassion, productivity, and blessings. Thank you, that you have called me to be a servant.

Thank you, that you bless the man who speaks of you and rewards them accordingly. Give me listening ears to hear a wise man's advice. Keep me from speaking unkind words, or foolish talk, or gossip, or slander, let me be prudent and overlook an insult. Keep my lips from dishonoring you. Give me a tongue that brings healing- speaking in love and truth. I know that you desire my heart to be honest, totally yours, and undivided - Grant that it may be — that I will not be deceitful, but that I will promote peace and joy.

Thank you for your protection that no harm falls on the righteous. Continue to protect your people. May you delight in your people, your Church, your Bride. May we honor you in words, thoughts, and actions. Help us be diligent in using our time wisely. May my speech be kind, encouraging, cheering others up.

Grant discernment in friendships, in all my relationships, that my influence may be Godly. Thank you for Jesus, who leads me in the way of righteousness, who gives eternal life. Blessed be Your Name.

In Jesus' Name

"Pour out Your favor and blessing... that I may please You!"

INSIGHTS IN CHAPTER 12

This chapter begins by acknowledging the one who loves discipline loves knowledge (v.1), and then in verse 2, the person who receives favor from the Lord, the Lord considers "good." Condemnation falls on the evil person—these contrasts between the righteous and the wicked continues in these verses. The writer brings out the truth, those who have the favor of the Lord, good things will fill their lives, and even their work reflects this (v.14)! It is very encouraging to know that as I seek God's wisdom and favor. He will bless me in such a way that my work will reflect His support! That is living wisely.

A Key Verse for this chapter is verse 2

"Good people obtain favor from the Lord, but he condemns those who devise wicked schemes." (NIV)

HELPFUL HINT: Try memorizing Proverbs 12:2 this week!

Proverbs 13.
The Fountain of Life

Dear Heavenly Father,

Thank you for the instruction from your
Word. May I hear you speak; may I listen to
your voice and obey your commands.

May I remember my father's wise
instruction and follow his words. Even
when I am corrected, may I search deep
within, confessing my sin, and allow Your
Spirit to cleanse and change me.

May my lips produce fruit that brings joy
and peace. May I guard my conversations,
help me think before I speak. May I again
only say what pleases You.

I desire to be diligent in my heart, so you
and your provision can satisfy me. Thank

you for your blessings. Thank you, that Your Spirit teaches the righteous to hate what is false and love what is right. Guard my life with your righteousness. Let no sin entangle me or cause defeat. Give me a heart that is honest, humble, and dependent on you.

Thank you, that You are my provider, whether I am rich or poor — may I trust in You. Shine brightly through me. May I have listening ears to hear wisdom's advice and follow it. Thank you that Jesus Christ, my Savior, satisfies the longings of my life. In Christ, there is life everlasting. Praise Your Holy Name.

Learning the teachings of the wise, understanding, and applying knowledge, my life will follow your commands. Give me the discipline to gather little by little and to be a good and faithful steward of your resources. May I bring healing and encouragement in all my relationships with others. Let me be receptive to correction and courageous to walk with the wise, that I may grow in grace.

You, Lord, reward the righteous, — please satisfy me with your blessing. Give contentment in your timing. Instill in me the ability to leave an inheritance for even my children's children — that this may bring a testimony of praise to You. Help me be a Godly parent, knowing when to discipline, when to correct, when to show love and compassion. Grant me words that will be receptive to my children's ears, that move them closer to You.

Thank you for all your blessings and for satisfying my mouth with good food to eat, filling my soul with the spring of Living Water. Blessed be your name.

In Jesus' Name

"Thank You that Jesus Christ Satisfies the Longings of My Life"

<u>INSIGHTS IN CHAPTER 13</u>

The contrast between the righteous and the wicked continues. Do you notice any other topics? Look for subjects such as; "poor and rich," "wise and foolish," "being a good steward," and "leaving an inheritance,", etc. What two words or verses "jumped off" the page and spoke to you? Could you write them as a brief prayer to God?

A Key Verse for this chapter is verse 14

"The teaching of the wise is a fountain of life, turning a person from the snares of death." (NIV)

HELPFUL HINT: Try memorizing Proverbs 13:14 this week!

Proverbs 14.
Building Life on Solid Ground

Dear Heavenly Father,

I thank you for the Godly women who build their house on their firm foundation of faith in you. Thank you for the wisdom that you give all of us. Thank you for the testimonies of those who walk in ways that are pleasing and upright before You. Their life reflects their love and respect for who You are. Thank you, you give wisdom to the wise so that their speech protects them in challenging times. Thank you for the wise steward who knows how to plan and produce an abundant harvest.

Even in troublesome times, those who are yours, you give them the desire to be a truthful witness— one who is honest and does not deceive.

Grant me a discerning and wise heart that I may not only find knowledge but discover true Godly wisdom. Your wisdom will keep me from going astray and falling for foolish things or following a dumb path. May your Spirit fill me with the "wisdom" of the prudent. Make my every step pleasing to You. Let your righteousness overflowing in me, cause me to be upright in your sight, and you bless me with your goodwill.

In those times that my heart faces bitterness, may You comfort me! May I seek you first in all I do, say, and think. May my life lived for you flourish. May I trust in Your way, Your leading, and not my "way," knowing that your way gives life, my approach will end in death. May I fear the Lord and shun evil, may my mind provide thoughts for my steps that bring obedience to You.

May your blessing, favor, and reward fall on me. I will declare your praises and bring honor to You. Thank you for the friends you have blessed me with. I am considered "rich" because of them. Help me be kind to the needy, showing Your love and faithfulness. Give me the discipline to work hard for You, that even my children may share in your wealth and be secure.

Thank you, that Jesus is my Living Water, a fountain of life to my soul. I praise You because You saved me from death. Grant me patience, understanding, peace, and contentment as I follow you. Your Spirit makes my bones come alive. Let me lift up Jesus Christ as my righteousness, exalting His name, showing His love and kindness, giving honor to You.

In Jesus' Name

"Your Wisdom will Keep Me from Going Astray and Falling for Foolish Things"

INSIGHTS IN Chapter 14

Take some time to compare the first 12 verses with Jesus' parable of the wise and foolish man found in Matthew 7:24-28. What do you notice? Who had the firm foundation? Faith in Jesus Christ is the believer's firm foundation (see 1 Peter 2:6, Ephesians 2:19-22). "Faith" grows by receiving wisdom from the Lord. Wisdom

strengthens Faith. To gain real "wisdom,"
you have to believe in Jesus Christ.

A Key Verse for this chapter is verse 27

*"The fear of the Lord is a fountain of life,
turning a person from the snares of death." (NIV)*

HELPFUL HINT: Try memorizing
Proverbs 14:27 this week!

Proverbs 15.
Peace Rules Over Anger

Dear Heavenly Father,

When I face harsh words or anger, grant me the ability to give a gentle answer. Help me respond to others with words of wisdom that promote your truth and knowledge.

I thank you because You are everywhere present at all times, keeping watch over the good and the bad. Your eyes see those things that please you and those things that grieve you. You truly detest the ways of the wicked, but love those who pursue righteousness.

May my actions please you. Help my conversations bring healing to others. Let my acts of worship be genuine, real, authentic, not hypocritical, not deceitful, and not puffed up. Forgive me of the times when I have grieved you. May I seek You with all my heart, all my soul, and with all my strength.

In honesty, humility, and deep reverence, I worship and honor you. Let me receive from your Holy Spirit the conviction and correction that I need to walk on the path of righteousness. Let me accept it with gladness, knowing you love those you discipline. Fill my heart with your Joy and love, knowing that as you do — even my face will be cheerful!

Thank you for the peace you give, that even if I have little, I can be content. Grant me patience, even during turmoil. Let your Word be a highway of life to my soul. Grant me understanding and the courage to ask others for their counsel and advice. Give me the right words to say to others at the right time, guiding me in my conversations with others. Let them find hope in you and trust you for living life abundantly.

Let me live honestly before you — knowing your Spirit searches the heart. May my thoughts be pleasing and pure. May my countenance even express your joy.

Thank you, that your word is "good news," thank you that the gospel is "good news," thank you for the privilege to share your "good news" with others! Thank you, that your truth brings health to my bones! Continue to speak to me, may I listen, trust, and obey you. May the fear of the Lord be my teacher of wisdom as I follow you. Thank you for your redeeming work in my life.

In Jesus' Name

"Let Your Word be A Highway of Life to My Soul!"

INSIGHTS IN CHAPTER 15

Have you ever spoken first, but wished you had listened? Solomon tackles dealing with harsh words, speaking without thinking, even dealing with anger in this chapter (see vv. 1, 2, 4, 7, 12, 17, 18, 23, 26, 28, 29, 30, 31). We need the wisdom to know what to say when to say it, how to say it and when to keep silent! Truly, a gentle response is far better than a harsh word.

A Key Verse for this chapter is verse 1
"A gentle answer turns away wrath, but a harsh word stirs up anger." (NIV)

HELPFUL HINT: Try memorizing Proverbs 15:1 this week!

Proverbs 16.
Commit Your Plans to the Lord

Dear Heavenly Father,

I thank you because you, Lord, respond to the plans of men. You see all, and you know all, you know my motives even when I can't see — you are faithful and allow my plans to be successful because I've committed them to you. May all that I do, say, and think in living my life bring honor and praise to you. May you work out everything in them for your glory. Keep me from a pride-filled heart. May your love and faithfulness surround me. Thank you for pouring your love through Jesus Christ by atoning for my sins. May I fall in reverence before Your Greatness. May I seek first your kingdom and righteousness, knowing that you give contentment and make my steps sure.

Pour out your wisdom on our leaders. May their mouths not betray justice or speak lies, but may they talk about the truth honestly before others. May you bless their leadership as they seek You and honor You. Pour out your righteousness that men's hearts will turn from wickedness to holiness.

May the joy of the Lord be our strength and song. You give life, may all who are yours reflect this. Grant us the desire for your wisdom more than any earthly treasure. Help us walk on the highway of the upright, guarding our life by your Word. Grant us humility and a teachable spirit.

May you bless all those who trust in you. May you fill us with wisdom in our hearts, may you consider us discerning, insightful, understanding, and encouraging. May our conversations be pleasant and bring healing to the bones. Keep us from following ways that lead to death. Help us walk on the path of righteousness. Thank you for giving us the desire to work, to have hunger - to help us be productive for you. Give us discernment and the courage to stay away from discord and gossip and violence.

Keep us from being swayed by smooth talkers who plot perversity and evil. Grant us patience and self-control. Give peace that we may live for you and attain a righteous life. May our lives be a crown of splendor, a testimony of your blessings. May I accept your decisions as I follow You.

In Jesus' Name

"Give Peace that we May Live for You and Attain a Righteous Life"

INSIGHTS IN CHAPTER 16

Chapter 16 contains many "golden nuggets" of wisdom. From committing one's plans, hopes, dreams, and motives to the Lord, and how should today's leaders lead? (See vs. 1,2,3,7,9, 12-15). Also, the writer reminds his readers that our speech should be sweet, gracious, and healing (vs. 21, 24). Better than the righteous have than all the wealth of the wicked (vs. 16, 19, 20). He even points out that patience in times of conflict is stronger than conquering a city (v.32). Ultimately, God is in control (v.33).

A Key Verse for this chapter is verse 3

"Commit to the Lord whatever you do, and he will establish your plans." (NIV)

HELPFUL HINT: Try memorizing Proverbs 16:3 this week!

Proverbs 17.
Wisdom Produces Peace

Dear Heavenly Father,

Thank you for the peace that Jesus Christ gives, which is not of this world. I am satisfied with little when your "peace" abounds. You bring calmness to my soul. Thank you.

You give wisdom to those who serve you by allowing them to have success even higher than those who hire them. You test my heart, may you find it pure and faithful to you. Help my ears to hear what is right and righteous; keep me from those who are malicious with their speech.

Let me be a person who is thankful, grateful to You for you are my Creator. I am

humbled and blessed to be created in your
likeness. Thank you for your blessings, for
giving me a family and letting me be a part
of a family.

Grant those who you appoint as our leaders
a truth-filled speech, keep them from bribes,
give them an honest heart. Let them show
forgiveness and hold no grudges. Allow
them to keep confidences and not betray
those who put their trust in them.

Keep me from folly, and rebellion,
reminding me that in doing so — it is like
trying to meet a bear and rob her of her
cubs; such behavior will only cause anguish
and harm. Let your peace permeate me in
such a way that I am a peacemaker, one who
ends quarrels and does not start them.

Thank you, that you see the hearts of men,
that you love righteousness, that you acquit
the innocent and condemn the guilty.
Thank you, that you paid the price of my
guilt through Jesus' death on the cross.

Because of Jesus, I can stand before you. I praise You for such a sacrifice, an offering of love. Grant me the desire for wisdom, to be a good steward, to be a faithful, loving friend, to deal with others honestly and with respect. Make my heart holy and righteous, cheerful, and not perverse.

Let my children follow you, your ways, and walk-in righteousness — keep them from foolish behavior and the means of folly.

Grant me a calmness, being even-tempered, being an encourager to others. Let me be able to hold my tongue and be discerning, especially in times of conflict. May I pursue your peace and may my life show that I love and follow You. Thank you for the grace and the gift of eternal life through faith — this wonderful gift from you. May I praise your name forever!

In Jesus' Name,

"Thank You for the peace that Jesus Christ Gives"

INSIGHTS IN CHAPTER 17

Several verses are favorites of mine in this chapter. Verse 9 speaks about the importance of love and how it can bring peace by covering offenses. Verse 17 talks about a "friend who loves at all times." To accomplish this, we need the Lord's love flowing through us. Verse 22 speaks about having a "cheerful heart." It is like medicine. We can uplift others with a joyful attitude and encouraging conversations.

A Key Verse for this chapter is verse 24 *"A discerning person keeps wisdom in view, but a fool's eyes wander to the ends of the earth."* (NIV)

HELPFUL HINT: Try memorizing Proverbs 17:24 this week!

Proverbs 18.
Wisdom Produces Strength

Dear Heavenly Father,

As I bow before You, I realize that you examine my heart and the hearts of all humanity. You know those who pursue selfish ends. Their conduct is unfriendly, and they are eager to start arguments and be divisive. I pray that you will bring your conviction upon them, that they may feel remorse and repent. So many are eager to speak their opinions and disregard others. So many people fill themselves with contempt and reproach. They do not know how to listen for the rushing stream of wisdom and hear your voice. They would rather cause strife than bring peace, cause pain instead of comfort, gossip instead of encouraging others. Move among your people that we may not be insensitive to others in our speech or conduct. Fill us with your words of love, truth, and wisdom.

You, Lord, are our refuge, our fortress, our strong tower. Thank you for your safety and protection. Thank you, that we can run to you in our time of need and you meet us and cause us to be safe. Thank You, that the path to righteousness begins with humility and not a prideful spirit. You exalt those who are humble and are your servants.

Thank you, Lord, for open doors of opportunity through generosity and kindness. Father, I ask that you move in people's hearts who are hurting, who are holding grudges and are unwilling to forgive. Bring healing to their souls. Let your word speak deep and fill their life with eternal truth and joy that it satisfies them. Give them a desire to hunger and thirst after righteousness.

Grant me the ability to speak your word that glorifies and honors you. Your Word is life, and those who receive it — live! Those who reject you usher in death. Oh, that you continue to pursue all who have a resistant heart that they may discover the power of Your love.

Thank you for blessing me with my family and my spouse. I praise You; it is a sign of your favor. Thank you for your faithfulness. Thank you for the body of Christ, the Church, my brothers and sisters in the faith—who stick closer than a brother.

In Jesus' Name,

"You lord are our refuge, our fortress, our strong tower!"

INSIGHTS IN CHAPTER 18

This chapter opens up and presents the painful agony of pursuing foolishness, selfishness, folly (see verses 1-8). Gossip and laziness are by-products of "Folly." These traits will not produce wisdom, and just the opposite will occur. The writer realizes that, "True wisdom" begins and continues to grow in the presence of God (v.10). The name of the Lord is a fortified tower and a strong fortress. There is safety in seeking the Lord, especially in times of trouble.

A Key Verse for this chapter is verse 10

"The name of the Lord is a fortified tower; the righteous run to it and are safe." (NIV)

HELPFUL HINT: Try memorizing Proverbs 18:10 this week!

Proverbs 19.
Living a Blameless Life

Dear Heavenly Father,

Grant me the ability by your Spirit to walk blamelessly, that my speech will be pure and true. Let me pursue your truth, give me the desire to know You more each day. Keep my heart from raging against you. May I not be swept away to ruin by folly. Grant me a spirit of self-control and not allow the things of this world like money or fame to push me away from You or others.

Help me be hospitable to others and generous, let my words be right, and reflect your wisdom. Help me be content in whatever state I'm in, relying and depending upon you. Thank you for your "wisdom" and understanding. Thank you for the new life that You give. Give me the ability to overlook an offense and grant forgiveness. Help me ask forgiveness if I have wronged anyone. May your favor and mercy fall on me. Keep me from being lazy, let me work with my hands as an act of worship to You.

Let me obey your teachings and your commandments. May they be a source of life and energy as I adhere to them. Give me a generous heart, to lend to others and be kind and help in time of need. Let me rest in your awareness of my actions, rewarding me accordingly.

Grant that I may be a better parent, able to teach, instruct, discipline, and correct my children as I seek to raise them in the ways of the Lord. Let me continually pray for them and their spiritual growth—that they may love you with all their heart, mind, soul, and strength and desire to live for You in this world.

In those moments when I need correction, help me receive it with humility and grace. Forgive me of those times when I resisted and did not listen. Give me ears to listen to advice and accept discipline, knowing that You are working all things for my good.

Father, place my feet where you want. Help me follow You. May my heart's desires reflect Your plans and purposes for me in this life. Thank you for your everlasting love. I bow in reverence and awe of You and who You are. Thank you for the peace You give. Thank you for the desire to please you in every way. Help me not bring shame to my family or my parents because of my actions. Give me a teachable spirit. May you reward me according to your lovingkindness and mercy.

In Jesus' Name,

"Give me the ability to overlook an offense and grant forgiveness"

INSIGHTS IN CHAPTER 19

This chapter highlights several areas where we need God's wisdom. We need His "wisdom" in our faith to walk with Him. We need his "wisdom" in dealing with others. We need His "wisdom" in accepting correction and giving forgiveness. We need His "wisdom" to work in our lives, to usher in peace. Take another look and ask the Lord how you can live your life, blamelessly.

A Key Verse for this chapter is verse 23

"The fear of the Lord leads to life; then one rests content, untouched by trouble." (NIV)

HELPFUL HINT: Try memorizing Proverbs 19:23 this week!

Proverbs 20.
The Shining Light of Wisdom

Dear Heavenly Father,

Keep my eyes focused on you. Let no alcohol or any other thing that tempts me, cause me to fall away from you. You are my source of joy in life. May I understand authentic leadership from your perspective and act accordingly. Help me avoid strife and become slow to get angry. Help me practice discipline and diligence. Thank you for giving work to humanity, so idleness and laziness do not become a way of life. Thank you, that you have a purpose for every human being. You give insight from your word. You draw out the very best in people. You give us the ability to be faithful because You are faithful. You give us the

ability to live righteous lives that brings
blessing to our children.

Your word is "true," there is no one
righteous, no not one. Yet, you forgive all
our sins. Thank you for forgiving me of all
my sins. Thank you, that you made me—
that you gave ears to hear and eyes to see.
Help me listen, follow, and obey you.

Help me be a productive and hard worker.
May I bring you glory through the work that
I do. When I speak to others, may my
words be knowledgeable and graceful! Let
me be honest in all my dealings, seeking
advice when needed, keeping confidences,
not talking too much, respecting others and
my parents and family. Grant me patience,
not clamoring for things or wealth. Let
your Holy Spirit satisfy every longing of my
soul. Let me be honest in all my business
dealings and transactions. Fill my life with
Your integrity, knowing that You direct my
steps.

Continue to shine your light on my heart,
that every word I say brings honor to You.
May your love increase and about all the
more to our leaders and everyone. Thank
you for the safety you give your people.
Thank you for the strength of the young
and the wisdom and splendor of the old.
Be glorified in my life. May I be able to
praise you in the storms of life. Do a
cleansing work on me. Be exalted
throughout our country.
In Jesus' Name

"You are my source of joy in life!"

INSIGHTS IN CHAPTER 20

This chapter brings practical insights into
everyday living. Notice verses 1, 3, 4, 11, 13,
18, 19, 22 and 25. From not letting Alcohol
rule your life to being honest in your speech
and disciplined in your work, the writer

encourages his readers to put into practice these steps to make one wise.

A Key Verse for this chapter is verse 27

"The human spirit is the lamp of the Lord that sheds light on one's inmost being." (NIV)

HELPFUL HINT: Try memorizing Proverb20:27 this week!

Proverbs 21.
It's the Matter of One's Heart

Dear Heavenly Father,

I thank you because you are Sovereign, and you are in control.

You determine leaders and their directions. Move among our leaders that they may please you in all they do and say. Thank you, that you are all-knowing — you know what is in our hearts. Help us do what is right and just for this pleases you more than sacrifices.

Remove pride and selfishness. Help us be diligent and to work hard. May my work ethic be an act of worship to you. Let my conversations be honest and truthful, dependable words built on Your Word. Let not violence and wickedness abound. Set free those who trap themselves by immorality and desire to do evil.

Thank you for noticing the widows and the orphans. Thank you because you have not left us abandoned or alone. Thank you, that you are just and give joy to the righteous. Help us stay faithful to your commands and be alert. Let the righteous flourish because of your blessing. Grant your peace in all marriage relationships that they may be a testimony of how Jesus loves the Church.

Let your righteousness and love be our goal, knowing that those who find it will find life, prosperity and honor. Give us the ability to be wise so we can go up against the city of the mighty.

Help us control our tongue and guard our mouths. Thank you because you give us the Spirit of self-control, you protect us from calamity. Thank you for the generosity of the righteous. May all who call upon your name find strength, discipline, and become hard-working—serving you with gladness and joy.

Let those considered upright give thought to their ways, to think before we speak, to believe, and step out in faith. Thank you again for your all-sufficient grace, your Almighty Power, and your Amazing love. I praise You because You Lord have won the battle, and victory rests with you.

In Jesus' Name

"Let your righteousness and love be our goal, knowing that those who find it will find life prosperity and honor."

<u>INSIGHTS IN CHAPTER 21</u>

This chapter highlights the rule and reign of God. God is Sovereign, and He knows all. He "weighs the matters of the heart" (v.2). God gives wisdom to the righteous and the wicked flounder. They are not prosperous (vs. 12, 16, 18). God is the one who grants peace in the marriage relationship and rewarding love (vs. 9, 19, 21). Take a moment and reread this chapter. Are you submissive to the rule and reign of God in your heart?

A Key Verse for this chapter is verse 21

"Whoever pursues righteousness and love finds life, prosperity, and honor." (NIV)

HELPFUL HINT: Try memorizing Proverbs 21:21 this week!

Proverbs 22.
The Source of a Good Name

Dear Heavenly Father,

My reputation relies and depends upon you.
It is more valuable than all the wealth in this
world. Please continue to build in me your
Christlikeness. Thank you, that you are the
creator of all of humanity. You give insight
to the prudent that they may see danger and
be safe. You give humility to those who
seek you, which produces wealth and honor
and life. You guide me on paths of
righteousness for your name's sake versus
leaving me to follow the ways of the
wicked. The wicked walk on roads covered
with trouble. Thank you, that you give
wisdom to Godly parents in raising their
children. Continue to help them teach and
model the love of Jesus to them. Let the

little ones come to know you, love you,
learn more about you, and desire to live for
you.

Help me be free from debts and free to
serve. Give me the ability to have no debt
outstanding except love. Help me sow
justice and truth and peace, not injustice or
calamity. Give me a generous heart and the
means to give away to others what they
need. Fill me with your Spirit that I may
overflow with love, joy, and peace. Create in
me a clean heart, a pure heart that I may
find favor in your sight. May your eyes be
pleased as you watch over me. Don't let my
foolish ways cause me to slip or fall, forgive,
rescue, and keep me from your anger.

Lord, give me ears to hear what your Spirit
is saying and teaching. May I pay attention
to your wisdom, and may I apply your word
to life. May your words saturate my
thinking so they become just a part of my
conversation and conduct.

Let me be generous to the poor and treat others with dignity, respect, and fairness. Help be honest and a good steward in all my financial dealings. Let me become skilled in my work that I may please you in what I do. May it be an act of worship that brings you glory.

In Jesus' Name,

"MY REPUTATION RELIES AND DEPENDS UPON YOU. IT IS MORE VALUABLE THAN ALL THE RICHES IN THIS WORLD."

INSIGHTS IN CHAPTER 22

This chapter finishes up the two-line proverbs and then starts with thirty wise statements (see v. 17 and following). Again, there is much wisdom and truth to learn. Topics include a "good" name (v.1), humility (v.4), raising children (v.6), rich vs. poor (vs. 2, 7, 26, 22) and others. Find one verse that speaks to you so you can apply to your heart and life.

A Key Verse for this chapter is verse 17

"Pay attention and turn your ear to the sayings of the wise; apply your heart to what I teach" (NIV)

HELPFUL HINT: Try memorizing Proverbs 22:17 this week!

Proverbs 23.
Be Content, Eager to Learn

Dear Heavenly Father,

Thank you for the opportunities you have given me to come my way. When I am in the presence of others, help me be content and thankful. Satisfy my hunger with the food placed before me. Giving thanks for the hands that have prepared the meal. Help me not give into cravings or coveting what others have.

Thank you, that you are my provider and source of all that I need. Let me remember that my wealth comes from you. You, Lord God, are my inheritance. The resources you have entrusted me with, let me be a good steward. Grant me a generous spirit and a loving heart.

Give me discernment when I am with others, keep me from being deceived when their loyalty to you is in question. Help me choose my words and conversations wisely and not waste them on those who will not listen. Grant me the ability, to be honest, to do the right thing, even if others do not. Let me speak the truth in love. Lord, apply my heart to your instruction and my ears to your words of knowledge.

Give insight and skill to all parents, that they may raise, discipline, and teach their children your ways, your truth. Let our children know you better and love you more deeply every day that you give them breath. Let their behavior be a testimony of their love for you and cause us to rejoice.

Protect us from jealousy and envy. Help us not want what others have or what others do. Create in us a clean heart. Give us a holy desire to be zealous for "the fear of the Lord." You, Lord, are our only hope.

Give me eyes to see the direction and steps you want me to walk. Keep me from the desires of this world, those who drink too much, those who overeat. Help my hands be diligent for the kingdom and not lazy, knowing that drunkards and gluttons become poor.

"Intoxicate me with Your love."

Thank you for my parents, for their example, for their love. Thank you, that you showed your love and grace to them. Thank you for the support and sacrifices they gave so I could prosper. Help me value their teaching, to see the truth in how they lived. Help me honor them by honoring you, gaining wisdom, instruction, and insight.

Father, take my heart, let my eyes delight in your ways. Keep me pure, holy, and free from the lust and desire for sexual sins. Let me be faithful to You and commit to being trustworthy in all my relationships. Let your Spirit lead me on the righteous path and not the wicked way. The wicked will reap sorrow, complaints, and strife. The righteous will know your joy, your peace, your contentment, filled with gladness. Keep my mind stayed on you, fill me with your Spirit, intoxicate me with Your love.

In Jesus' Name,

INSIGHTS IN CHAPTER 23

Themes covered in these verses are contentment, thankfulness, parenting, honesty, envy, purity, honoring God with what I eat, say, and do!

A Key Verse for this chapter is verse 12
"Apply your heart to instruction and your ears to words of knowledge." (NIV)

HELPFUL HINT: Try memorizing Proverbs 23:12 this week!

Proverbs 24.
The Wise Versus the Foolish

Dear Heavenly Father,

Help me not envy the wicked, nor desire their company; for their hearts plan violence and their conversations always focus on making trouble.

Let me focus on seeking wisdom, using your truth to build my house on a firm foundation. Grant me understanding and knowledge from your Word that I may apply it to my life. You fill my life, like a house filled with treasures, with great wealth from your teachings.

You give power and strength to the wise. Guidance to those who seek information and victory to those who gain it. Help me ask for advice, especially in the conflicts of life. Grant me "Holy Spirit Strategies" that I may see, hear, implement, and do your will, your way, for your glory.

Help me know and see the folly of my ways, let me not judge others when they exhibit foolish behavior, but let me teach them in grace and in a speech that shows "tough love."

In your Holy Word, You have revealed the ways the foolish. They are schemers, mockers, weak, being led away to slaughter like livestock. They stumble and fall. Calamity comes upon them, and eventually, their light is gone. Lord, help me pray for my enemies, not celebrate or rejoice when they stumble or fall. Help me grieve with those who mourn and rejoice with those who "rejoice."

Grant me reverence and respect for you, my God. Help me be an example to others of one who loves you with all my heart, soul, my mind, and strength. Let me be one who loves my neighbor as myself. Help me be a good citizen and submissive to those you have placed over me in leadership. Grant me the ability to show no partiality to others, to be fair and honest, not discriminatory, that it may go well with me. Let my speech be honest and my message well received.

Lord, remove in my life the temptation of laziness. Help me show diligence and discipline. Help me always work in your strength, praying, planning, preparing, and producing good "fruit" that will endure my lifetime. Bless my home as a witness of your blessings. Bless my work, that it may be a testimony of your kindness. Keep me from poverty, and may I be grateful for all that you have given me and are doing for me.

In Jesus' Name,

"Grant me understanding and knowledge from your Word that I may apply it to my life."

<u>INSIGHTS IN CHAPTER 24</u>

Here, the writer compares the wisdom, true statements of the wise versus the evil, foolish ways of the wicked. It is better to know and understand the pitfalls of foolishness and the blessings of wisdom. "Strive to be wise, and your house will be built (v.3-4)."

A Key Verse for this chapter is verse 14

"Know also that wisdom is like honey for you: If you find it, there is a future hope for you, and your hope will not be cut off." (NIV)

HELPFUL HINT: Try memorizing Proverbs 24:14 this week!

Proverbs 25.
Digging for Gold

Dear Heavenly Father,

Your ways are higher than a man's ways!
You have hidden the mystery of the ages of
humanity from humankind. You have
allowed your servants and kings' to discover
your truth down through the ages. You
have miraculously revealed your plan of
redemption through Jesus Christ. Thank
you, that you have not treated us as our sins
have deserved, but loved us so much by
giving new life to all who believe in your
only Son.

Thank you, that those who seek you, find
you. Those who search for profound truth,
you, by your mercy, reveal hidden gems.
You remove the impurities from our lives.
You establish kingdoms and nations that
flourish through righteousness. Make our

nation righteous in your sight. Grant
blessing to our leaders — may they seek
your wisdom and glory more than anything
else. Allow humility to raise and exalt the
leaders of your choosing. Help me be
patient in the process of leadership. Let me
rest in your choosing.

Give me the ability to keep confidences, not
to reveal a secret, that others will know I
can be trustworthy and dependable. Grant
me the understanding to give good advice
and to receive correction when needed.
Help me be faithful in giving words to
others that will refresh them in spirit. Let
my words be encouraging, gentle, and
persuasive in times of need. Let me be
reliable, honest, and sensitive to others.
Help me minister as Jesus would.

If my enemy is hungry, help me give him
food to eat, if he is thirsty, help me give him
water to drink—knowing that you will
reward me. Let me leave the outcomes of
conflict with you. You are our provider and

peacemaker. When others look at me, may they see Christ's reflection! When others hear me speak, may they hear Christ's words as a fragrance of praise and wisdom! Keep me from being sly, deceptive, or hurtful to others in what I say. Let your peace permeate my home. May my house be a place of hope and joy. Help me stand for truth and righteousness and bring good news. Let me not compromise your gospel message. Grant me a spirit of self-control and discernment, that my actions may honor you always.

In Jesus' Name,

"Those who search for deep truth, you, by your mercy, reveal hidden gems."

INSIGHTS IN CHAPTER 25

This chapter highlights more wise sayings of Solomon by "the men of" King Hezekiah of Judah. Notice most of the verses are in two phrases. Each phrase or statement gives a different perspective of each wise saying. For example, verses 16-17, the warning is don't eat a lot of honey, or you'll get sick. Compare this to overstaying one's welcome in your neighbor's home, "Too much of you, and they will hate you!" What other comparisons can you find?

A Key Verse for this chapter is verse 2

"It is the glory of God to conceal a matter; to search out a matter is the glory of kings." (NIV)

HELPFUL HINT: Try memorizing Proverbs 25:2 this week!

Proverbs 26.
The Fool, Sluggard, & Maniac!

Dear Heavenly Father,

Help me not be like the fool who craves for
honor and attention but does not earn it or
deserve it. There is no sense of peace or
self-control for one who is foolish.
Discipline cannot even correct a fool; they
sear their understanding of learning. Help
me show wisdom in the company of fools,
to not respond to their folly. Let their ways
not influence me — let me not compromise
when I am eager to help when giving advice.
Help me remember it is like "cutting off
one's feet or drinking poison" (v. 6). Let
my speech focus upon your Holy Word. Let
my words thrash not as a thorn bush but
bloom as a bountiful harvest. Keep me

from pride, let me be humble and seek mercy as I serve you.

Give me the discipline to speak the truth in love. Your word is useful and profitable for correction, rebuke, instruction, and training the righteous man. Not like the sluggard who is undisciplined and yells about danger, but does not know or senses when real danger comes. Give me eyes to see this world the way you Lord God sees this world and obey accordingly. Create in me a strong work ethic. Keep me from being lazy. Grant me a teachable spirit and an attitude open to understanding. Give me listening ears to hear and fill me with your Spirit. Allow me the calling to be a peacemaker, not an argument starter.

Let me love my neighbor as myself as you love them. Help me genuinely care for others' needs and not joke or ridicule or laugh at others for my enjoyment. Forgive me of the times when I think I am better than anyone else. Let my words be few and help me show self-control even in the most trying of times.

Create in me a clean heart not bent on evil, but an undivided one, fixed on Jesus Christ only. May my lips reflect the sweetness of Christ's words. May my enemies deceitful ways expose them. Convict them of their sin. Treat them according to your Sovereign justice.

Thank you for the assembly of your people, may your presence fill each heart as they gather. May your splendor adorn each soul as they seek you. May your Spirit search hearts, cleanse, and forgive sin, empower every believer to live for you as they worship. Keep your people from gossip, from lying, from flattery, and fill their tongues with those things that are true, noble, right, pure, lovely, admirable, excellent, and praiseworthy (Phil. 4:8).

In Jesus' Name,

"Allow Me the Calling to be a Peacemaker not an Argument Starter."

<u>INSIGHTS IN CHAPTER 26</u>

I would summarize this chapter on how to deal with the fool (vv. 1-12), the sluggard (vv. 13-16), and the Maniac (vv.17-28). All three reveal that their heart is bent towards evil and wrongdoing. Pride has overcome them! The wise is humble and acts the opposite of the wicked. Take notes as you read and search your heart, do you act like one of these three? Ask the Lord to help you act wisely in all your relationships and decisions.

A Key Verse for this chapter is verse 12
"Do you see a person wise in their own eyes? There is more hope for a fool than for them."(NIV)

HELPFUL HINT: Try memorizing Proverbs 26:12 this week!

Proverbs 27.
God Will Take Care of Tomorrow

Dear Heavenly Father,

Help me not worry about tomorrow or brag about tomorrow because today has enough trouble of its own. I confess I do not know it all, and I do not know what tomorrow may bring. Help me trust you fully today and tomorrow. Let me not push my reputation or agenda but wait on you — letting others praise me.

When I get angry or provoked, let it come from a heart founded and built on righteousness, not foolishness. Let me receive correction and rebuke openly. Let me learn from the wounds and honest help from my friends and not reject their counsel. Let me be content with what I

have and not hoard, but share with others in
their need. Let the advice of friends be like
a fragrant perfume that is pleasing and
causes joy. Let me receive it with
thankfulness.

Help me be faithful to my friends and
family. In times of trouble, let me be
sensitive and go to those who will help me
instead of being a burden to my family or
friends. Help me bring joy to you as a son
brings joy to their father, who obeys him.
Let me be discerning of the times and sense
danger and take refuge. Keep me from
being blinded by not being aware and sober-
minded.

Bless my marriage that my relationship with
my spouse will be one of peace, love, and
joy. Let me hear and focus that our
conversations will encourage each other.
Grant, in us the ability to walk agreed, to
stand firm together in the storms of life and
to complement, not irritate each other.
Grant us the wisdom to help each other

become stronger. Make us a couple who please you by building others up and encouraging them in your ways. Look at our hearts and let our life reflect you, Lord Jesus.

While we live on earth, satisfy us with your Holy Spirit's presence. Give us contentment because of your grace and provision. Let our words stand firm, centered upon your truth.

Give me the ability to be a good shepherd, like Jesus. Let me know the condition of my flocks and give careful attention to their hearts. Let me put my trust in you—for in you; there is security. Thank you for your watch-care and provision for me, not only today, but for tomorrow. I praise your Holy Name.

In Jesus' Name,

"While we live on earth, satisfy us with your Holy Spirit's presence."

INSIGHTS IN CHAPTER 27

This chapter touches on the rightful place of boasting (v.1) and how to gain praise — let others do it (v.2). Notice verses 5,6,11,14,15,17, and 21—all deal with one's speech and conduct. The chapter concludes with insights for those in pastoral ministry today (see vv. 23-27). There is a blessing when one knows "the condition of their flocks."

A Key Verse for this chapter is verse 17

"As iron sharpens iron, so one person sharpens another."

HELPFUL HINT: Try memorizing Proverbs 27:17 this week!

Proverbs 28.
The Rich and The Poor

Dear Heavenly Father,

Help me be "as bold as a lion." Help me be a victorious champion of the faith, to stand for truth on the battlefield, and give courage to those around me. Help me wear your whole armor (Ephesians 6) as you give victory. Give the leaders in our country discernment and knowledge of how to govern in these days. Let them not oppress the poor or forsake instruction or not understand what is right. Let them seek you wholeheartedly.

Let me be content with the little that I have. Keep me from coveting what the rich may have. Help me foresee the destruction of sinful lifestyles. Let me show discernment

and the application of instruction in my life.
Give me the ability to be a good steward
who is kind and generous, especially to the
poor.

Let my leadership be without fault. Give
me the insight to choose the right path to
walk and lead others on it. Not one that is
evil, but one you have designed. You lead
us on paths of righteousness for your
names' sake.

Grant victory to those who are righteous, let
me celebrate with those who overcome.
Keep me from the wicked—protect your
people. I fall in reverence, awe, and tremble
before you. My heart is tender and
teachable. Show me your ways. Protect us
from trouble, helplessness, tyranny, hatred,
and murder. Keep our walk blameless and
safe.

Instill in me the desire to work hard, to be
productive, to gain abundance, and not
chase fantasies. Let me know the difference

between chasing fantasies and following your dreams and plans for me. Give me your patience as I follow you, building faithfulness and trust. Help me be true to you even if I'm hungry — let me not betray you.

Make my conversations be like a healing balm, rebuking and correcting those who need correction, building up, and encouraging those who need your love. Grant me a generous heart. Help me honor my father and mother by bringing peace and unity in my family and not disagreement or selfishness. Let me not take advantage or steal from my parents, but help them as an act of worship to you. Let me support them, showing how grateful I am.

Let me trust in you and not myself. As you look at me, let my motives be pure, peaceful, and loving. Guide my feet to walk in wisdom, giving generously to the poor. May your blessings and favor and riches fall on

me, and may I honor you as your faithful
servant.

In Jesus' Name,

"Let me celebrate with those who overcome."

INSIGHTS IN CHAPTER 28

There are several comparative statements
mentioned in this chapter that echo
elsewhere. What does it take to live a
righteous life? Read this chapter and write
verses that help answer that question.

A Key Verse for this chapter is verse 5

*"Evildoers do not understand what is right, but
those who seek the Lord understand it fully."*
(NIV)

HELPFUL HINT: Try memorizing
Proverbs 28:5 this week!

Proverbs 29.
When the Righteous Thrive

Dear Heavenly Father,

Grant me a willing heart, a teachable attitude, a desire for learning, and doing what is right. Keep me from being obstinate and stubborn. Let me thrive as one of your righteous children so that others will rejoice. Do not let the wicked rule.

Give me a love for wisdom that brings joy and provides security. Instill in me, the desire for truth and justice. In all my dealings with people, help me be honest. Help me pray for my neighbors and not deceive them. Let your joy overflow that I shout with gladness because you call me righteous! Let me love and care about

justice for the poor, turning away anger with
peaceful words and actions. Protect me
from those who seek to kill the upright.
Remove the spirit of hatred and murder
from those who are against your children.
Instill in us, the integrity of your Word.
Grant us safety as we proclaim your truth.
Even in times of danger, help us be brave,
bringing calmness to the conflicts we face.

Give us your eyes of discernment to see the
signs of the times and know how to live.
Grant our leadership the ability to make fair
laws and decisions. Grant parents the ability
to impart wisdom, teaching, and disciplining
their children in ways that bring honor to
the whole family. Let their children rise and
provide "the delights" that they desire. Let
your peace be the calming influence and let
your love be the motive.

Give us eyes to see your revelation and
vision, practicing restraint when needed,
obeying wisdom's instruction. Help me
think before I speak, to pull my "fair share"

of the work-load, to be a peace-maker and not one who stirs up conflicts, or is "hot-tempered."

Let me gain a greater understanding of the danger of pride, how it brings a person low. Let me learn humility and strive to be low in spirit. May I bring glory to your Name.

Keep me from being a partner to anything or anyone who desires to do evil. Let me trust and fear you, Lord, more than humanity. You designed my steps long ago, may I rest in your wisdom and may you fulfill your will for my life. Help me promote honesty and righteousness as I live for you.

In Jesus' Name,

"Give me a love for wisdom that brings joy and provides security."

<u>INSIGHTS IN CHAPTER 29</u>

Again, this chapter highlights many comparisons — answering the question "how to live a good life!" The advice the writer gives is priceless. Notice verses 2 - 6, just for starters — as you read, write those verses that speak to you. Notice that the righteous thrive (v.2), care (v.7), the righteous see the wicked's downfall (v.16), and they detest the dishonest (v.27).

A Key Verse for this chapter is verse 18

"Where there is no revelation, people cast off restraint; but blessed is the one who heeds wisdom's instruction." (NIV)

HELPFUL HINT: Try memorizing Proverbs 29:18 this week!

Proverbs 30.
Learning Wisdom

Dear Heavenly Father,

I confess, sometimes I grow weary and tired. I become low and believe I lean on my understanding instead of trusting in your wisdom. Forgive me of those times when I have not learned your truth, your wisdom, the lessons you are trying to teach me. Give me the discipline and desire to attain understanding and insight into the "knowledge of the Holy One." Not for posterity's sake, or prestige, but from a heart devoted to you.

Only your Son Jesus has ascended to heaven and come down to earth. Only you, Lord, have gathered up the wind! You've made the heavens and the earth. You wrap the waters up like a cloak. You established all the ends of the earth! How amazing You are! "What is his name, and what is the

name of his son? Sure, you know!" Yes,
Your name is higher than any other Name -
Your Name - Yahweh, Your Son Jesus, God
my Father and Son Jesus Christ, who have
given us Your Holy Spirit, the teacher,
counselor, and comforter. You alone are
God. Who am I that you should even
notice me?

Yet you are my shield, and your word is
flawless, your "word" is right. We can add
nothing to Your Holy Scriptures, for they
are complete. As the writer of these
proverbs desire to have lies far from him
and have only his daily bread provided, so
too, Lord keep me from dishonest lips and
lies, provide for my daily needs. Let me not
bring you shame by my thoughts or
behavior. May I never turn away from you
and your love. May I never dishonor your
name.

Help me treat others with your kindness and
respect. Let me honor my parents by living
for you—bringing praise to you from what

they have taught me. Cleanse me from all
sins, give me a humble spirit, and sees me
the way you see me. Let your love be my
weapon as I live for you.   Grant
contentment and satisfaction with things
too wonderful to comprehend. Help me be
thankful for seeing you work miracles in
surprising ways.

"Give me the desire to attain understanding and insight of 'the knowledge of the Holy One.'"

Lord, may I discover the wisdom of the ant,
to store up food for the winter, being
disciplined and diligent — these days.
Grant me a Christ-like character, that
testifies of the Lion of Judah, who is
victorious overall. Let me rest in you and
not play the fool, nor exalt myself, nor plan
evil — let me pursue wisdom, humble as a

servant, seeking righteousness. Let my steps promote peace; this, I pray.

In Jesus Name,

INSIGHTS IN CHAPTER 30

This chapter introduces us to another writer of Proverbs, Agur, son of Jakeh. Some believe that Agur was a wise sage during Solomon's time, while others think it was an Arabian Wiseman. He states that he isn't smart (vv. 2-3), but he reveals wisdom from God (vs. 5-6). He gives practical advice — see verses 7-9, 10, 11-14, 15). As you meditate on this chapter, you will gain many insights.

A Key Verse for this chapter is verse 5

"Every word of God is flawless; he is a shield to those who take refuge in him." (NIV)

HELPFUL HINT: Try memorizing Proverbs 30:5 this week!

Proverbs 31.
A WIFE OF NOBLE CHARACTER

Dear Heavenly Father,

Help me listen to your Holy Spirit speak to me through the pages of Your Word. May I focus and spend my strength on things that please you, energizing me to accomplish your will. Keep me from the things that will take me away and cause ruin in my life. Let me not love this world nor the things of this world (1 John 2), but let me love you with all my heart, my mind, my soul, and with all my strength (Matthew 22:37). Help me speak up for those who cannot speak for themselves — primarily when prompted by You. Help me defend the rights of the poor and needy and to be fair in my opinions. Change my thoughts and

attitudes — may they conform to your
divine thinking.

Thank you for the example of a Godly wife,
described as noble, which is far more
valuable than rubies. Her testimony speaks
of her dedication to you, and through her
actions, she shows her love to you, her
husband, her family. In all she does —
from her decisions to her accomplishments
— she brings a fragrance of praise because
she is trusting in her God completely.
Thank you, that her husband has confided
in her, that she brings him good all the days
of her life. Thank you for the wisdom that
you give her, as she carries out her daily
duties—she provides food for her family
and is wise with her money. You give her
strength and an abundance of energy in
fulfilling her work.   Her heart is generous
and kind. You enable her to provide for her
family. Because of her — the city respects
her husband. She exhibits strength, dignity,
laughter, wisdom, faithful words that teach
as she lives her life. Her children speak her

praise and bless her. Her husband honors and cherishes her, praises her for all that she does.

Lord, this is not a fairy tale; this is attainable for all women who marry and have put their faith in you as Savior and Lord. You give the secret of wisdom — it is "fearing the Lord" in one's heart. You bring praise to those who do this. Lord, I pray that you will bless every Christian marriage, may this be their testimony. May you bring harmony, unity, love, and honor to all who trust and fear your Holy Name. May you honor the Godly women in our day. Fulfill your purpose for us, your people. May "your will be done on earth as it is in heaven," for your glory.

In Jesus' Name,

"Thank you for the example of a Godly wife."

INSIGHTS IN CHAPTER 31

King Lemuel records his wise sayings. Notice verses 8-9, "Speak up for those who cannot speak for themselves"... and then he concludes with the most famous verses of all the Proverbs, Proverbs 31:10-31, a wife of noble character. If we're honest, most women today may resent this portion of scripture. While most men would hope for a wife described like this! So - stop. For a moment, ask the Lord, what does He want you to see from these verses? A person who dedicates herself to her God and through this commitment is faithful to her husband and family. That is a testimony all of us can have as we seek to walk in the Holy Spirit, dependent upon God in everything we do. He is the giver of wisdom! Just ask Him!

A Key Verse for this chapter is verse 30

"Charm is deceptive, and beauty is fleeting, but a woman who fears the Lord is to be praised."
(NIV)

HELPFUL HINT: Try memorizing Proverbs 31:30 this week!

Epilogue.
A life-Time pursuit

Dear Reader and Intercessor,

You've made it through the 31 prayers of Proverbs! Congratulations! Let me encourage you to take some next steps!

STEP 1 - Memorize each of the weekly Scripture verses.

STEP 2 - Make these prayers your own. Better yet, write prayers with your own words based on scripture!

STEP 3 - Explore other passages of God's Word to pray. For example — the Psalms! Or Pauline Epistles!

STEP 4 - Share these prayers with someone and even pray with them!

STEP 5 - Make your prayer time a regular part of your Bible study and devotions. Revisit these prayers often. Let the Lord build in you His Godly wisdom.

Seeking God's wisdom is not just a "one and done," deal. It is a lifetime pursuit. I encourage you to keep on asking and seeking the Lord. Keep knocking on God's door. Remember what Matthew 7:7-8 says, "Ask, and it will be given to you; seek and you will find; knock, and the door will be opened to you. 8 For everyone who asks receives; the one who seeks finds; and to the one who knocks, the door will be opened." (NIV)

Jesus tells us that persistence pays off! The one who keeps on asking, keeps on seeking, keeps on knocking, guess what? God will answer their prayers. God will give them what they ask. They will find the answer, and God will open the door! God will answer your prayers in His time according to His will and purposes for His glory. So keep being diligent and keep believing, trusting, and praying. The Lord God will meet you. Your prayers are a fragrant offering unto Him (Revelation 5:8, 8:3-4). I can't wait to hear one day — all that God has accomplished — because you asked Him!

"MY REPUTATION RELIES AND DEPENDS UPON YOU. IT IS MORE VALUABLE THAN ALL THE RICHES IN THIS WORLD."

ACTION STEPS

Take a moment and look again at steps 1 - 5, which one will you begin with this week? Make a plan, pick one or two, and when you will start. Make a date to meet with the Lord in prayer each day. He will meet you as you spend time with Him.

WHICH STEP?

_____

WHAT'S YOUR PLAN?

_____
_____
_____
_____
_____
_____
_____
_____

WHAT DATE WILL YOU START?

_____

About the Author

Teddy James O'Farrell is a Pastor, Teacher, Writer, Musician, Guitarist, Songwriter, and Worship Leader. He attended Nyack College and Rutgers University. At Liberty University, in Lynchburg, Virginia, he earned an M.A. in Music & Worship. He is happily married to his wife, Susan. They make their home in Zephyrhills, Florida. They have three grown adult children and one adorable granddaughter. He also enjoys a good cup of "coffee."

For More Information:
www.teddyofarrell.com
or www.zaccma.org

www.ingramcontent.com/pod-product-compliance
Lightning Source LLC
Chambersburg PA
CBHW060018050426
42448CB00012B/2800